Welcome to Busy Book 4!

Can you find these things in the book? Write the page number in the star.

The Busy Book helps children develop in the following areas of learning…

 Communication
Learning to speak together in English.

 Leadership
Learning to build relationships.

 Discovery
Building knowledge and awareness of social responsibility.

 Critical thinking
Solving problems and puzzles and learning thinking skills.

 Creativity
Expressing ideas through drawing and making.

 Self-management
Learning to plan ahead to reach goals.

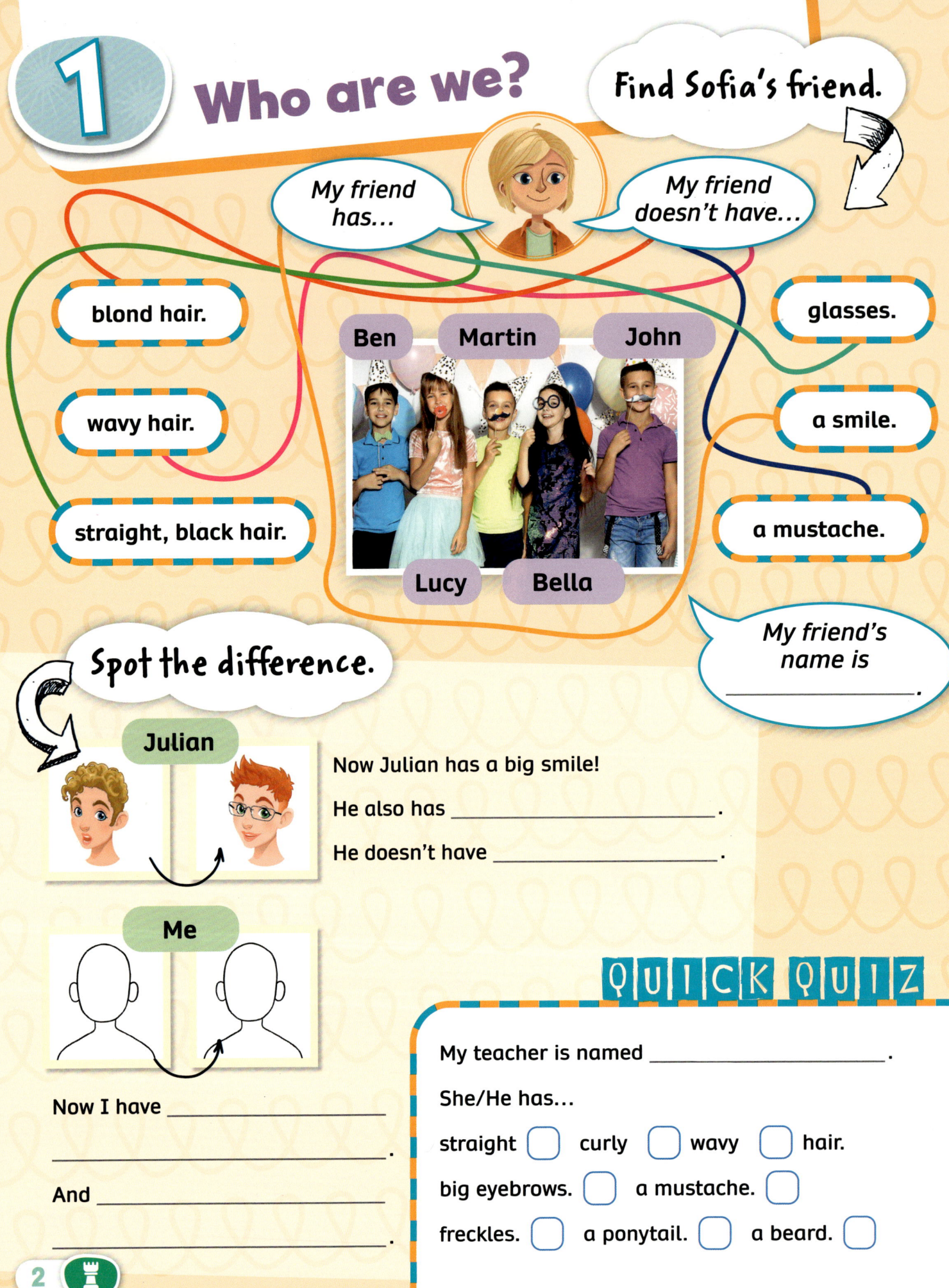

Imagine with Hugo
Who has the necklace?

Read and complete.

CITY NEWS

STOLEN NECKLACE!
The police are looking for a special necklace. They have a letter with some information. "There are a lot of numbers," says Detective Smith, "but we don't understand it!"

a=26, b=25 ➡ y=2, z=1

WHO HAS THE NECKLACE? THE PERSON HAS...

4 26 5 2 / 19 26 18 9   w a v y / h a i r.

13 12 / 25 22 26 9 23   n o / b e a r d.

25 18 20 / 22 26 9 9 18 13 20 8   b i g / e a r r i n g s.

26 / 25 9 26 24 22 15 22 7   a / b r a c e l e t.

Can you help the police?

Use the code. Complete the letter. Who has the necklace?

___Eva___ has the necklace.

Invent your own code. Write a message to a friend.

a	b	c	d	e	f	g	h	i	j	k	l	m	n	o	p	q	r	s	t	u	v	w	x	y	z

3

Guessing game

Complete and play the "Who is it?" game.

Alex	Lisa	Carla	Charlie
Marcus	Juan	Anna	Mei
Ben	Kwame	Lucy	Tom
Nick	Katie	Asim	Daisy

Katie has long, wavy hair and earrings.

Tom has short, straight hair and glasses.

Sorry, I don't understand. Can you say that again, please?

Is it a girl?

Yes.

Does she have long hair?

No, she doesn't.

Is it Lisa?

Yes, it is!

Tongue twister

Can you say this quickly five times?
Smart Sam has short, straight hair!

Explore with Eva — Our world

Match the drums to the countries.

"I always play my cajon. It's a special drum from Peru. Sometimes I play with my friends."

"We often play our drums in competitions."

"We never feel sad when we play our drums!"

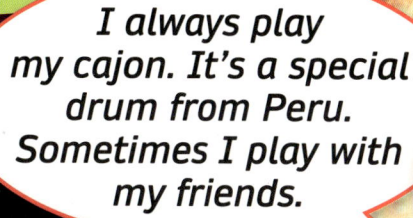

Nigeria

Scotland

Explore more

Find out about more drums from around the world. Draw.

Find someone who has one of these special things.

☐ drum   ☐ necklace   ☐ bracelet
☐ earrings   ☐ coin   ☐ blanket

_____'s special thing is a _____.

It's _____

_____.

5

My funny characters

Choose and draw your characters.

princess	police officer	blond	green	hair	earrings
superhero	server	straight	pink	eyebrows	a blanket
funny animal	bus driver	curly	yellow	mustache	a necklace
spy	doctor	wavy	red	nose	a bracelet

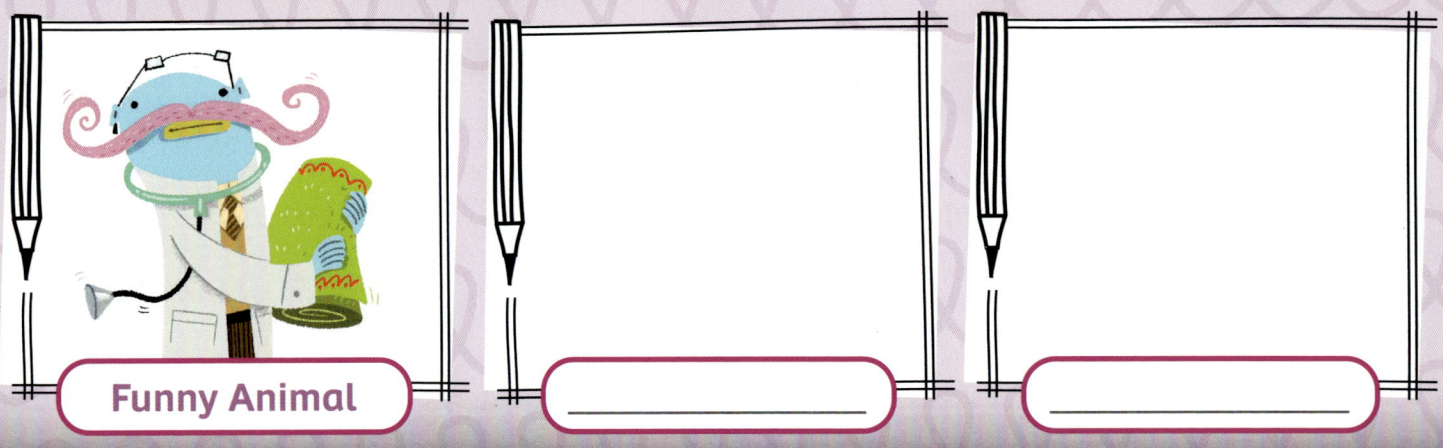

Funny Animal

My characters are named _____ and _____.

_____ has _____ but doesn't have _____.

_____ has _____ but doesn't have _____.

My favorite activity in this unit:
_____

My new words:
_____
_____

I will find out more about:
_____
_____

Can you write a story about your characters?

Let's use it again!

Count the words and color.

- ☐ boxes
- ☐ cups
- ☐ bowls
- ☐ rugs

Use a mirror and match.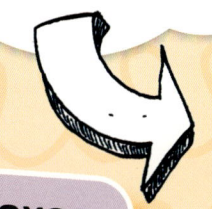

sweater
jacket
plate
purse
shelf

QUICK QUIZ

Name something you put…

on a plate.	_____
in a purse.	_____
on a shelf.	_____
in a box.	_____

Imagine with Hugo

What's in the box?

Read and complete the story.

Millie and Jack are in a dark room in an old, scary house.

"Look at those boxes on that old, metal shelf!" says Jack.

Millie opens the first box. "This is a rubber duck."

Jack opens the second box. "These are plastic cups and glass plates. Nothing special."

Millie opens the third box. Under some brown paper, she finds something very special.

"Look, Jack! Whose _____ _____ are these?"

"They're yours now! And mine!" says Jack.

"Excuse me... they're MINE!" says _____ !

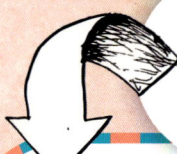

Use these ideas or your own.

metal   rubber   plastic
wood   paper   glass

coins   necklace
pictures   paintings

Draw a picture of the ending of your story.

8

Island hop

You will need: a spinner, two game pieces

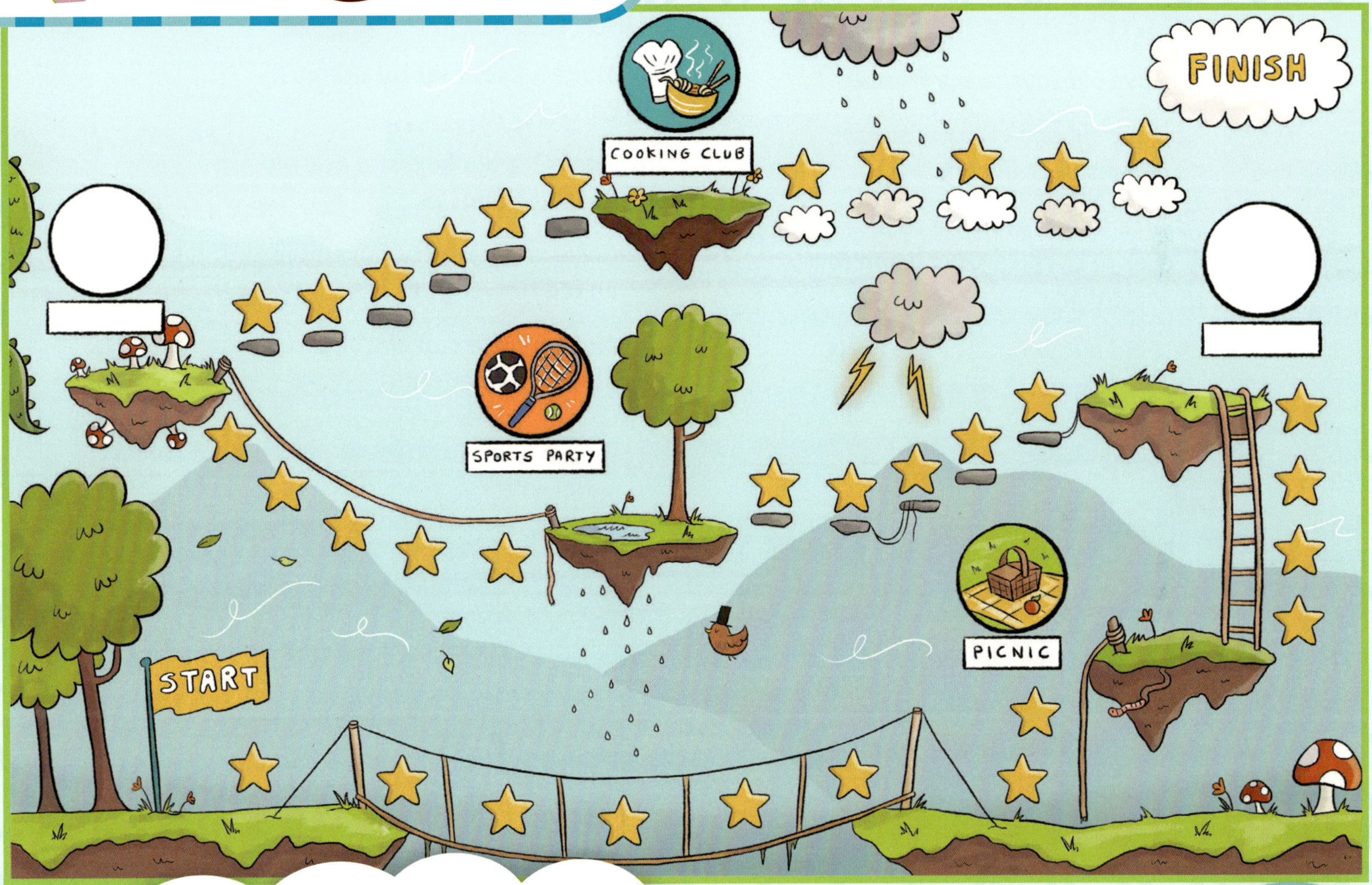

Take turns to spin the spinner. When you get to an island, or go past one, invite your friend.

COOKING CLUB

SPORTS PARTY

PICNIC

START

FINISH

Add your own two islands to the game.

Would you like to come to *a picnic*?

Yes, please. I'd love to!

No, thanks. Sorry, I can't!

Tell me a joke!

What goes up, but never comes down?

Your age!

9

Explore with Eva — Our world

What can I do? Check (✓).

RECYCLE

1. Give old toys to my friends. ☐
2. Give old books to my school, hospital, or library. ☐
3. Use things at home to make a huge box of cookies. Give them to a neighbor. ☐
4. Find out where I can recycle glass, plastic, and paper. ☐

UPCYCLE

5. Make a list of metal things I can upcycle. ☐
6. Decorate old boxes to put my special things in. ☐
7. Grow some pretty flowers in an old flower pot. ☐
8. Make a little cup out of a plastic flower pot. ☐

At home, I recycle...	paper	metal	plastic	wood	rubber	glass
always						
often						
sometimes						
never						

Explore more

Where can you recycle things in your town or city?

the recycling center   the grocery store
the town square   home   school   the community center

I can recycle _____ at _____.

My upcycling ideas

Can you find old things in your home to upcycle?

Draw or stick pictures.

Use your old things. Design an upcycled gift for a friend.

I can upcycle these rubber boots to make flower pots!

I can upcycle _____
_____
to make
_____.

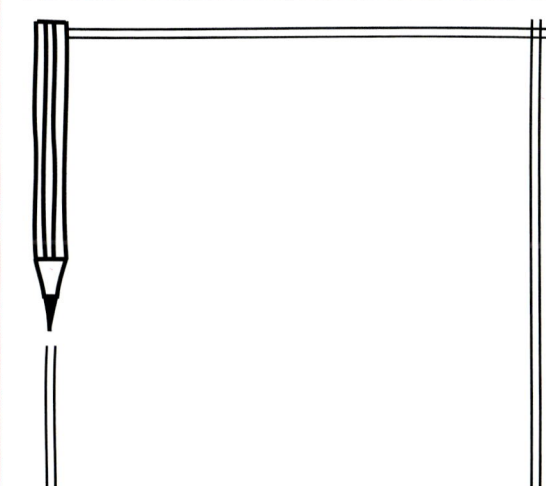

My favorite activity in this unit:
_____

My new words:
_____
_____

I will find out more about:
_____
_____

3 City of the future

Complete the wordsearch.

Look for the city words!

skating rink   mall
amusement park
stadium   restaurant
~~art gallery~~   swimming pool

A	M	U	S	E	M	E	N	T	K	L	Y	G	K
P	A	R	K	P	T	F	D	L	L	I	N	J	Y
K	L	S	W	I	M	M	I	N	G	E	O	F	E
E	L	O	S	T	P	O	O	L	W	I	S	T	L
Q	B	W	T	U	O	D	Q	Y	F	R	K	O	Q
I	K	O	A	R	E	S	T	A	U	R	A	N	T
W	J	K	D	A	R	T	K	W	P	O	T	R	Y
A	G	F	I	G	A	L	L	E	R	Y	I	I	W
P	L	Q	U	B	N	L	O	D	L	R	N	N	O
R	O	U	M	N	W	F	M	O	L	F	G	K	W

Think and write.

 +  +  + 🍳 + 🐞 = h _ _ _ _

Draw a code for a place in town. Ask a friend to guess.

QUICK QUIZ

I can see…

special paintings at the _____.

fun rides at the _____.

popular shows at the _____.

amazing soccer players at the _____.

Imagine with Hugo — **Fun in the city**

Draw the animals. What do they like doing?

Hippo

At the amusement park, Hippo likes going on a ride.
"I enjoy it because it's fun!"

At the stadium, Tiger likes watching a game.
"I like watching the soccer players run!"

Tiger

At the theater, Lion loves watching a show.
It's something he always enjoys.

Lion

Monkey likes going shopping.
He loves looking at all the toys.

Monkey

Penguin likes going to a restaurant.
He goes with his friends from the pool.

Penguin

And at the museum, they love exhibits,
they're interesting, fun, and cool!

Your turn!

Draw or stick in a picture.

I like going _____

because _____.

I also like _____

_____.

13

Maze challenge

Find the gold.

Instructions:
Draw five more gold coins on the board. Play a game with a friend. Tell your friend where to go.

Turn left.

Turn right.

Go straight on.

Stop!

Choose your challenge!
Find all the gold and get to the FINISH in
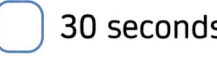 5 minutes. 2 minutes. 30 seconds.

Riddle
Where am I?
The first part sounds like *apartment* and the second part sounds like *shark*.

Our world

Explore with Eva

Let's do a city tour!

Choose your tour. Check (✓).

I like…

▲ new things. ☐	● acting. ☐	■ ice cream. ☐
■ sports. ☐	▲ having a picnic. ☐	▲ sharing. ☐
■ exciting places. ☐	■ being outside. ☐	▲ cute things. ☐
▲ being with my friends. ☐	● old things. ☐	■ playing soccer. ☐
▲ pizza. ☐	▲ clothes. ☐	● painting a picture. ☐
● learning. ☐	● interesting places. ☐	● being inside. ☐
■ scary things. ☐	● being by myself. ☐	■ going on adventures. ☐

Which tour is your favorite? Count.

☐ ■ **Fun outside:** Do you like activities that are exciting, fun, and sometimes scary? Let's enjoy going on rides at the amusement park or watching a game at the stadium!

☐ ▲ **Food and friends:** Do you like having fun with your friends and sharing new things? Let's enjoy going to restaurants and going shopping at the mall or at the market!

☐ ● **Culture:** Do you like learning, watching things, and visiting interesting places? Let's enjoy watching shows at the theater and going to exhibits at the museum!

Explore more

Think about places in your town or city. Then write.

I like _____ because it's lovely.

I like _____ because it's clean.

I don't like _____ because it's boring.

I don't like _____ because it's dirty.

I like _____ because it's _____.

_____ because it's _____.

My city break

Create the perfect city day trip for friends or family.

I'm creating a Saturday city trip for
_____.

Show at 7 p.m. every Saturday.

Exhibit open 9 a.m. – 5 p.m. on the weekend.

Soccer game on Saturday at 7 p.m.

Open daily 10 a.m. – 8 p.m.

Saturdays 8 a.m. – 1 p.m.

Open 8 a.m. – 8 p.m. on the weekend.

Ask your friends or family what they like doing before you plan.

Write and draw or stick pictures.

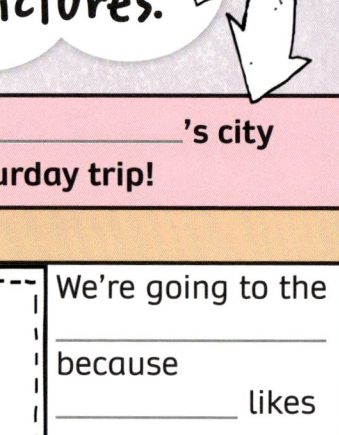

_____'s city Saturday trip!

Morning

We're going to the _____ because _____ likes _____.

Afternoon

We're going to the _____ because _____ likes _____.

Night

We're going to the _____ because _____ likes _____.

My favorite activity in this unit:
_____

My new words:
_____
_____

I will find out more about:
_____
_____

Food for everyone!

Count the foods to complete the crossword puzzle.

Circle the one that doesn't belong.

- pasta   lemons   rice   bread
- pineapples   grapes   potatoes   apples
- milkshake   water   orange juice   beans

QUICK QUIZ

What's your favorite…

fruit? _____
vegetable? _____
drink? _____

The hidden fruit is: ☐☐☐☐☐

Imagine with Hugo: The Rainbow Cafe

Choose and write. Then draw your funny cafe, the server, chef, and the food!

astronaut	dolphin	teacher	funny animal	inventor
happy	scary	huge	cool	special
soup	rice	pasta	pizza	honey
box	bag	cup	glass	bottle
olives	lemons	pineapples	vegetables	potatoes
sofa	plate	bicycle	shelf	blanket
two	five	twenty	fifty two	a hundred

Welcome to the Rainbow Cafe!

Our chef is a _____ _____ who can make _____ _____ dishes for you.

Sit on a _____ and choose your food. Our _____ server brings all the dishes on a _____. There's a lot of _____ with _____ and _____. There's also some _____ with a lot of _____ and _____. Is there any waste? No, there isn't! Not at our _____ cafe!

Come on your birthday and we give you a _____ of _____ and _____ _____ in a _____ to take home!

Tell your friends and family about your cafe!

How much is it?

Ask, remember, and answer!

Instructions:

1. Player 1 looks and remembers the prices.
2. Player 2 hides the picture from Player 1 and chooses a food to talk about.

Player 1: *How much is it?*

Player 2: *It's €1.50.*

Player 1: *Sugar?*

Player 2: *Yes! My turn.*

SUGAR €1.50
FLOUR €1
JUICE €3
POTATOES €2
GREEN BEANS €1.25
HONEY $2.50
GRAPES $2
PINEAPPLE $1
PASTA $1.50
LEMONS $1.25

Tongue twister

Can you say this quickly five times?

Sit down now, big brown cow!

Explore with Eva: Our world

Let's make lunch! I have...

- a bowl of **beans**
- some **bread**
- a cup of **rice**
- a lot of **carrots**
- a box of **tomatoes**

Spain: paella

Eva can use _____.

U.K.: sandwich

Eva can use _____.

Japan: bento box

Eva can use _____.

Mexico: pico de gallo

Eva can use _____.

Explore more

What dish can you make from your country using Eva's food? Draw and write.

I can use _____

to make _____.

QUICK QUIZ

To not waste food, I like to…

… make ☐ a smoothie. ☐ a cake. ☐ lemonade. ☐ chips.

… share with friends. ☐ family. ☐ _____

My pizza menu

Design pizzas for a new restaurant!

My no-waste list

a bag of _____

a piece of _____

a box of _____

a bottle of _____

a _____ of _____

a _____ of _____

On my pizza menu, there's…

_____

_____

There aren't any…

_____

_____

Can you make your pizzas at home?

My favorite activity in this unit:

_____

My new words:

_____

_____

I will find out more about:

_____

_____

Pizza menu

Pizzas

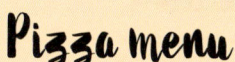

_____
$_____

_____
$_____

_____
$_____

Drinks

a glass of   a cup of

_____   _____

$_____ $_____

5 Help our oceans!

Match and draw.

1. snail 2. jellyfish 3. octopus

What are the animals doing? Check (✓) or put an ✗.

CLUES

The sharks are swimming in the cave. They aren't in the plants.

The crab is on the rock. It isn't sitting.

The dolphins are in the ocean. They aren't hiding.

The seahorse is in the plants. It isn't playing.

The starfish are sitting. They aren't in the cave.

playing	✗				
swimming	✓	✗	✗	✗	✗
sitting	✗				
walking	✗				
hiding	✗				
in the ocean	✗				
in the plants	✗				
on the rock	✗				
at the beach	✗				
in the cave	✓				

The sharks are __swimming__
in the _____.
The _____ are
_____.
_____.
_____.

QUICK QUIZ

Guess who…

has a curly shell? ☐ snail ☐ seahorse

is a fish? ☐ whale ☐ shark

can grow a new arm? ☐ seal ☐ starfish

Imagine with Hugo

The big beach clean-up

Read, draw, and write.

Hi! I'm at the beach with my community group. We're having a beach clean-up. Our work helps to clean the oceans.

There's a lot of plastic at the beach. It's very dirty! My friends are helping me to pick up trash.

Look! There's some plastic, glass, _____, and _____ . These pieces of trash are damaging our oceans. But we can recycle them.

How many yellow plastic bags of trash can you see in the story?

We're making a movie to tell people about our beach clean-up. Are all my friends looking at the camera? Yes, they are! Smile, everyone!

1, 2, 3... What can it be?

Draw the activities.

Nature trail
Day: Tuesday
Place: the park
Time: four o'clock

No plastic bag day
Day: Wednesday
Place: the mall
Time: ten o'clock

Ocean picture exhibit
Day: Wednesday
Place: the mall
Time: one o'clock

Upcycling day
Day: Thursday
Place: the mall
Time: ten o'clock

No-waste picnic
Day: Friday
Place: the park
Time: one o'clock

Octopus dance party
Day: Saturday
Place: the beach
Time: ten o'clock

Beach clean-up
Day: Saturday
Place: the beach
Time: one o'clock

Tree planting club
Day: Saturday
Place: the park
Time: four o'clock

Clean water day
Day: Sunday
Place: the beach
Time: ten o'clock

Ask a friend to choose a card. Ask them 1, 2, or 3 questions. Then guess.

- When is it?
- It's on Saturday.
- Where is it?
- It's at the beach.
- What time does it start?
- It starts at one o'clock.
- Is it the beach clean-up?
- Yes!

Tell me a joke!

How do dolphins go to school? By octo**bus**!

Explore with Eva

Our world

Our ocean in numbers

1. How much of our world is ocean?
   - [ ] 10%   [ ] 50%   [ ] 70%
2. What is the largest ocean animal?
   - [ ] lemon shark   [ ] blue whale   [ ] bottlenose dolphin
3. We use over 500 billion plastic bags a year. That's…
   - [ ] 15   [ ] 150   [ ] 1500   bags for every person on our planet!
4. How many pieces of plastic go into our oceans every day?
   - [ ] 8 million   [ ] 20 million   [ ] 100 million
5. How many baby sea turtles have dangerous plastic inside them?
   - [ ] at least 20%   [ ] at least 60%   [ ] at least 80%

Our brilliant oceans have a problem: plastic pollution. What do you know about this topic?

Explore more

What trash can you find near your home? Can you use it to make art?

This crab was made with plastic bottle tops.

Draw your Trash Art or stick in a picture.

Be safe. Use gloves when you pick up trash.

My ocean tour

Imagine an ocean tour. What can you see? Draw and color.

Can you talk about your tour for one minute?

How much is your tour?
When does it start?
What are the animals doing?
Is your ocean safe or dangerous?
Is it clean or dirty?

My favorite activity in this unit:
_____

My new words:
_____
_____

I will find out more about:
_____
_____

Write about your picture.
Does it have an important message?

In my ocean tour, there is a
_____ and there are some
_____ .
_____
_____
_____
_____
_____

Let's play together!

Write and color.
Then complete and draw.

 ☐☐☐☐☐☐☐  ☐☐☐☐☐☐☐☐☐☐

 ☐☐☐☐☐☐☐☐☐  ☐☐☐☐☐☐☐☐☐

 ☐☐☐☐☐☐  ☐☐☐☐☐☐☐☐☐☐

 ☐☐☐☐☐☐☐☐  ☐☐☐☐☐ ☐☐☐ ☐☐☐☐☐

Color red, blue or orange for play, go, or do.

☐☐☐☐☐b☐☐☐☐☐☐☐☐

QUICK QUIZ

I like… ✓ but I don't like… ✗

☐ playing volleyball.   ☐ playing badminton.   ☐ going snowboarding.
☐ playing ping-pong.   ☐ playing baseball.   ☐ going swimming.
☐ playing field hockey. ☐ doing track and field. ☐ _____.
☐ playing basketball.   ☐ doing gymnastics.   ☐ _____.

Imagine with Hugo

Rabbit and Crab

Read the story.

Rabbit and Crab are going to have a race to the ocean.

"What are you going to do, Crab? Are you going to run?"

"No, I'm not. I'm going to fly!"

"You're going to fly?"

"Yes, I am!"

"I'm going to win the race!"

Rabbit thinks she's the winner. But Crab is flying!

Rabbit is jumping hurdles. She isn't looking behind her. But Crab has Rabbit's tail.

"Where are you, Crab?"

"I'm here! I'm going to go swimming!"

"You're too smart for me, Crab!"

Imagine you're an animal. Choose who you want to play a sports activity with. What are you going to do?

lion   monkey   parrot   tiger   penguin
whale   dolphin   mouse   chicken

throw a ball   bounce a ball
hit a ball   run   jump hurdles   fly

I'm a _____ and I'm going to _____, with a _____ !

Explore with Eva

Our world

Find your unusual sport!

- Are you going to play ball sports?
  - Yes → Are you going to go to the ocean?
    - Yes → Can you jump?
      - Well → **Pirate Volleyball** — Pirates love playing beach volleyball. The winner gets gold coins!
      - Badly → **Octopus Tennis** — Playing tennis with an octopus is fun. It has a lot of arms to hit the ball quickly!
    - No → Can you bounce a ball?
      - Badly → **Octopus Tennis**
      - Well → **Space Basketball** — Do you want to play basketball on the moon? It's very cool. The ball can bounce high!
  - No → Do you like animals?
    - Yes → Can you run?
      - Quickly → **Snail Races** — Slowly... slowly... a snail race can take hours, but the snails are very cute!
      - Slowly → **Dragon Races** — Dragon racing is an exciting sport for brave people. Don't fly badly or you will fall off!
    - No → Are you going to play exciting, scary sports?
      - Yes → **Dragon Races**
      - No, thank you! → **Sleeping Competition** — Just pick up a pillow and close your eyes. Sleep well!

Explore more

Think of a sporting hero. Find out three facts about them.

Name: _____   Sport: _____

FACT 1: _____

FACT 2: _____

FACT 3: _____

My sports team

Imagine a new sports team!

Team name: _____

Our sport: _____

Our players: ☐ my friends ☐ superheroes ☐ animals ☐ _____

Player names: _____
_____

Our team shirt: Our team badge:

My special team

My new sports team is named
_____.

We are going to
_____
_____
_____
_____.

My favorite activity in this unit:
_____

My new words:
_____
_____

I will find out more about:
_____
_____

31

 **Goodbye**

About me

I like this book because...
_____
_____ .

My favorite activities in this book are...
_____
_____ .

Something I'm going to remember from this book is...
_____
_____ .

Rise and Shine Certificate

You finished Busy Book 4!
Good job!

Awarded to: _____
Age: _____   Date: _____

Sofia   Hugo   Marco   Eva   Zoe   Socks